Our Two Gardens

Margaret Hebblethwaite anc Peter Kavanagh

OLIVER-NELSON PUBLSHERS

Nashville

We have two gardens, and I love them very much.
One is quite small, and is behind our house.
I share it with my family.

The other garden is big.
I share it with everyone in the street.
And I share it with everyone in the country.
And I share it with even more people than that.

2

This must be a very big garden! It is bigger than you can imagine. It is as big as the world. In fact, it is the world.

The world is a garden, planted by God. God is the best gardener there has ever been.

3

God planted trees and grass and bushes,
and from them come fruit and flowers and food.
The garden is full of millions and millions of different
kinds of growing things. They all grow because God
has given them the rich earth and the warm sun,
the fresh air and the wet rain.

God also made streams and rivers and waterfalls and seas.
All the best gardens have water in them. And God
made fish to swim in the
waters — everything
from sardines to
whales.

And God put
beaches by
the sea
where you
can lie in the
sun and play
in the sand.

5

God didn't make the garden all flat and the same,
but full of different kinds of places.
It is great fun to explore.
Some parts are cold, like the north and south poles,
where there is a lot of ice, and the top of mountains,
where there is snow. I have seen photos in my book
about mountains.

Other parts are hot, like the thick rain forests, where the trees are full of bright birds and buzzing insects.
I have seen pictures in a magazine my father gets.

In our little garden we also have trees —
an apple tree and a tree with a swing.
We have grass for playing on, and we have a flower bed.
There are also a few vegetables like lettuce and carrots.

We even have a fish pond in our little garden.
There is a small, hilly rock garden.
And there is a little greenhouse all made of
glass for growing special plants and flowers.

So our little garden has trees and fruit,
grass and food, water and fish, rocks and
hot places, just like our big garden.

9

Our little garden is good for playing little games.
But if I want to play big games I go out somewhere
in our big garden, like down to the river.

I think, 'All this is mine,' because God made it for me
and for everyone else too. It is ours to play and work
and sit in. It is ours to explore for as long as we want.

And it is not just for everyone in the world now,
but also for all the people who have not yet been born.
It is for everyone until the end of time.

When we moved to our house we were happy to find it had
such a lovely little garden. We liked everything we found there,
and we hoped it would stay just as nice as when we moved in.

But after we had lived here for a year or two we saw that
things were going wrong. There were fewer apples on the tree.
The flowers and vegetables didn't grow so well.
The grass was worn and had bare patches.
Some of the plants in the greenhouse were dead.

And the air in the greenhouse made you feel sick. There were weeds spreading all over the flower beds and we tried to get rid of them with weed-killer.
My sister and I had left bottles and soft drink cans on the vegetable patch.

There were plastic bags and torn newspapers blowing over the rock garden.
The fish in the pond were dead, and the water was slimy and smelly.

I no longer wanted to play in our little garden.
One day the man next door leaned over the fence and said,
'Your garden used to be so beautiful, and now it is quite spoiled.
You should do something about it.'

My parents were very embarrassed.
'What should we do?' they said,
'We do not have much time for gardening.
Who could get it right again?'

He said, 'You should call the gardener who used to look after it before
you moved in. Here is the telephone number.'

My father rang up, and the next week the gardener arrived. Her name was Nancy. She had soft brown hair and wore green rubber boots. We all liked Nancy because she made us feel it was fun to look after our little garden.

When Nancy began to work she said to us,
'This soil is very bad. You have spread too much weed-killer, and it has poisoned the earth. You will be able to grow good flowers and vegetables again, but we will have to wait a while.'

Then I began to notice that things were going wrong in our big garden too. Down by the river some of the tree tops had lost their leaves, although it wasn't autumn.

'They are being poisoned too,' Nancy said.
'Their poison comes in the rain, which is polluted by power stations and factories and car exhausts. It is called acid rain.'

Nancy drained all the water from the pond because that was poisoned too, and no fish would live in it. She planted a little water weed and put in some water snails to keep the water clean.

'Now we can put in more goldfish,' she said, 'and they will live here happily.'

I told Nancy that when we first moved here, people used to fish down on the river bank. But no one goes there to fish any more, and the water has a creamy scum on it.

'The water is polluted now,' she said. 'There is a sewage farm upstream and it sends out such a lot of filth that fish cannot live in the water. In some countries people have to drink water like that. It makes them ill, and many of them die.'

Nancy went around picking up all the
bottles and cans and plastic and
paper that we had left lying around.
I went to help her. So did my sister.

We were proud when we saw
how nice we were making it.
With three of us working it did
not take long.

20

When we lifted the lid off the bin, Nancy said, 'Look at all the potato peelings and cabbage leaves you have thrown away.'

'If we make a compost heap with this vegetable matter, we will have some rich compost to spread on the earth. That will help the apple tree to grow better fruit.'

Nancy showed us what to do for the future. 'These bottles should be taken to be recycled,' she said. 'The glass can be broken down and melted and made into new bottles.'

'You may be able to recycle the cans too, especially if they are made of aluminium.'

'These plastic bags are a nuisance and should be put in the bin. But it is better to get paper bags or biodegradable bags, which will break down in the earth eventually.'

'The newspapers should be kept dry and tied in bundles, so they can be made into recycled paper. Then not so many trees will need to be cut down to make paper.'

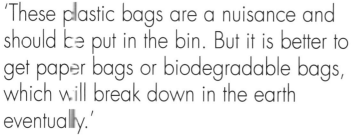

23

Then Nancy explained that the grass was worn in the places where we played most often. 'It does not have a chance to grow,' she said.

'As soon as a new shoot comes up you stamp all over it.' She sowed new seed on the bare patches.

Then she tied string around so we would remember to leave it alone to grow.

The next day we had a lesson at school about deserts.
The teacher told us that every year more land turns into desert
because people use the same patch of ground so often
that nothing will grow there any more.

'Yes,' said Nancy, 'where there is desert, the people can't grow food.
You also get a desert when the trees are cut down and the wind
blows away the top soil that used to be held in place by their roots.
Many animals and insects and plants are dying where the trees are
cut down. The people who live in the forests are dying too, because
they are losing their homes.'

Then Nancy went into the greenhouse. 'This smells disgusting,' she said. 'It smells as if someone has been sneaking into the greenhouse to smoke cigarettes.'

We all looked at my mother and she turned red.
'We will have to leave the door open for a couple of days to get the air clean again,' said Nancy.

I told Nancy that when my father took me to the city the air there also smelled nasty and made me feel sick.

'That is because of the cars,' said Nancy. 'The exhaust fumes are very bad for us, especially if the cars do not have catalytic converters.'

27

'The plants in here,' Nancy went on, 'are dying because they don't have enough water. It is nice and warm in the greenhouse, but the soil dries out more quickly. You must water them more often.'

I told Nancy I had heard of something called the greenhouse effect, and I asked her what it was.

'The world is getting hotter,' she said. 'Too much coal and oil is being burned, and that sends gases up into the air which hover like an invisible ceiling of glass. Then the heat from the world is trapped, as though we were in a huge greenhouse. Some countries are going to get so hot and dry that the crops won't grow, and there will be famines.'

'Near the north and south poles the ice will begin to melt in the warmer air. The sea level will rise, and many people who live near the sea coast will have their homes flooded.'

921044

Now at last Nancy has made our little garden as beautiful as it was before. When I come home from school I run out to play. I am so looking forward to being in our garden.

And the man next door tells us, 'Now I love to look out of my bedroom window and see your beautiful garden.'

But when will our big garden be put right? I think it is time the leaders of the world got embarrassed and did something about it.

Then once again the trees will grow, and the fish will swim in the waters. The fields will be green and the people will have enough food. Those who live in the forests will have a home once more, and those who live in the cities will breathe fresh air at last.

Then all the children who have not yet been born
can look forward to living in our big garden.
They will find it fun to play and work and sit in.
They will explore it for as long as they want.

They will eat good food and drink clear water.
They will be healthy, and the world will be full of life and laughter.
And that is the way God meant it to be.